D1313643

KARATE BASICS

KARATE BASICS

J. Allen Queen

Sterling Publishing Co., Inc.   New York

Edited by Claire Bazinet
Photography by Samuel Jones, III
Artwork by Lynn Andrus

Library of Congress Cataloging-in-Publication Data
Queen, J. Allen.
    Karate basics / J. Allen Queen; photography by Samuel Jones, III;
drawings by Lynn Andrus.
        p.   cm.
    Includes index.
    Summary: Introduces the art of karate, discussing workout space,
clothing, safety, nutrition, related rituals and exercises, and the
stances, punches, kicks, and blocks.
    ISBN 0-8069-8676-X
    1. Karate—Juvenile literature. [1. Karate.] I. Jones, Samuel,
ill. II. Andrus, Lynn, ill. III. Title.
GV1114.3.K436   1992
796.8'153—dc20   92-25112
                                                               CIP
                                                                AC

10 9 8 7 6 5 4 3 2

First paperback edition published in 1993 by
Sterling Publishing Company, Inc.
387 Park Avenue South, New York, N.Y. 10016
© 1992 by J. Allen Queen
Distributed in Canada by Sterling Publishing
℅ Canadian Manda Group, P.O. Box 920, Station U
Toronto, Ontario, Canada M8Z 5P9
Distributed in Great Britain and Europe by Cassell PLC
Villiers House, 41/47 Strand, London WC2N 5JE, England
Distributed in Australia by Capricorn Link Ltd.
P.O. Box 665, Lane Cove, NSW 2066
Manufactured in the United States of America
All rights reserved

Sterling ISBN 0-8069-8676-X Trade
              0-8069-8677-8 Paper

To my sensei, Carl

Acknowledgments

Special thanks to Robert Wingo III,
Melissa Whitley, Sean Kime, Scott Myers,
Heidi McLeod, Holly McLeod,
Mallice Felder, Alexander Queen,
Alex Mauney, and Charlie Mauney
for their assistance in
making this book possible.

CONTENTS

1 BEGINNING KARATE 9

2 THE WORKOUT 17

3 THE BASIC STANCES 39

4 OFFENSIVE KARATE 51

5 DEFENSIVE KARATE 67

6 SPORTS KARATE 91

7 QUESTIONS & ANSWERS 121

INDEX 127

1
BEGINNING KARATE

You have probably seen karate performed in the movies or on television. Maybe you have even rented videotapes so that you could match real or cartoon characters, over and over again, throw punches and kicks at the bad guys, defeating two or more attackers at the same time. You may even have imitated the karate fighters, throwing kicks, punches, or chops around the room complete with bloodcurdling screams that sent the family dog running. Yes, you will find punches, kicks, and sounds associated with violence in the art of karate, but you will also find strength, discipline, respect, courage, and a sense of self-control if you learn karate correctly. Most of all, you will gain self-esteem and feel confident in the face of challenge.

Is Karate for You?

Is karate for you? Only you know. Karate is not for everyone. You will have to exercise, eat properly, and practise daily. That can be hard, but the rewards are great. Nobody can express the feeling of pride and happiness that will come over you as you tie that coveted black belt around your waist for the very first time. Don't you owe it to yourself to

find out? There is no such person as a natural in karate. Anyone can learn this exciting sport. Anyone. Even you! So get ready to experience one of the greatest art forms and sports in the world.

Your Workout Space

Now that you have decided to learn karate, your next step is to prepare your workout space. While you will not need a great deal of space, you will want an area that will allow you to do warm-ups, kicks, punches, and practise other karate techniques. A large room or part of a garage is quite acceptable. When the weather permits, using the backyard or patio area for karate practice is fine.

You may even be able to use your own room. For most of your exercises and karate techniques you will need enough space to be able to stand and stretch your legs forward, backwards, and to both sides without hitting anything. A space six feet by six feet should be sufficient for now.

What to Wear

You might like to purchase a karate suit called a gi (pronounced *gee*) to wear at your workouts. Karate suits come in an assortment of different colors and styles. Colors include the traditional white, black, red, blue, and denim. Styles include the standard suit with drawstring pants and wrap-around jacket, and suits with lace-up pants or elastic-waistband pants. Some also use short "sport" jackets. Although an authentic karate suit will give you a greater sense of being a karate student, a regular sweat suit or oversize pants and shirt will be fine to work out in. Karate suits can be ordered from companies that advertise in major karate magazines, or from some sport stores.

The cost of student uniforms is usually in the $20 to $30 range. Later on, you may want to purchase hand and foot gloves for sparring.

Warm-Up Exercises

In the study and practice of karate, warm-up exercises are not only just a good idea—they are the building blocks to becoming a good martial artist. You will find karate exercises much different from any of those you have done for other sports, such as football, tennis, or running. The major purpose of the exercises, other than to simply warm up so that you won't hurt yourself, is to stretch your muscles so that you will have more flexibility, and to give your kicks greater height. Exercises are also important for balance and strength.

Follow the instructions carefully, when doing the exercises shown later in this chapter. Never "bounce" or force yourself to stretch or reach so far that it causes pain. It takes time to retrain the muscles for karate practice. It would also be a good idea to check

with your doctor to make sure that you are in good health before you begin a program of karate training. If you take this book along, you will be able to show the doctor the types of things you will be doing.

Safety

One of the first rules of karate is never do anything that will hurt you or anyone else. Getting a medical checkup is a good first step. Unfortunately, as with any sport, accidental injury is always possible. In order to minimize the risk of any accidental injury, it

is always important to be careful in all aspects of karate practice. This includes warm-up exercises, practising kicks, blocks, and punches, and especially when you are sparring with another student. In beginning karate, you never actually hit another person. The only time a punch or kick should land is if you are really being physically attacked. As you continue to study the art of karate, you will learn how to deliver a crippling or deadly blow to defend yourself if your life is in danger.

Karate students, however, learn to control their kicks and punches, to deliver a kick to the chest or a punch to the head to within one inch of the target. It is this control that will allow you to practise karate safely and to take part in the sport aspect of sparring. The ability to control the placement of

punches and kicks to a sparring partner, a punching bag, or a dangerous attacker is called focus. You will learn more about focus as you learn karate kicks and punches.

Nutrition

Eating the kind of foods to keep your body in good condition is very important. Foods rich in complex carbohydrates will give you the energy you need to exercise and work out properly. These foods include potatoes, rice, dried beans, noodles, corn, beets, and other vegetables. Raw fruit such as apples, bananas, and pears are additional sources of complex carbohydrates.

To keep muscles and bones growing strong, while controlling your weight, eat healthful proteins such as are found in fish, chicken, turkey, and lean beef. Drink plenty of low-fat milk for calcium. Get your vitamin B from eating breads, cereals, and grains at every meal. These will keep your body functioning well. Fresh fruits and fruit juice are good sources of Vitamin C, which will help defend your body against germs and diseases. Roughage, found in most salad ingredients, is good for you too. Remember to drink plenty of water daily. Your body needs lots of water in order to digest and get the most from the foods you eat. If you work out for long periods of time, your body will "ask" for more water by making you feel thirsty. Your doctor can tell you more about your specific nutritional needs based on your age, size, weight, and other factors that can influence your diet.

Self-Esteem

Do you know how good you feel about yourself when you hit a home run in a baseball game, win a race, or get a good grade on an especially hard test? That good feeling is

13

point, in order to improve or gain more skills, you decide that you need to practise more. The discipline to practise when you would rather be doing something else is being responsible. By disciplining yourself, you learn the importance of devoting the time and effort you need to succeed. As you become more responsible, you will notice others, especially people who matter in your life, reacting positively to your growing maturity. With appropriately developed skills, gained confidence, and learned responsibility, you will have achieved a positive self-image and a healthy sense of self-esteem.

self-esteem. Self-esteem is how you value yourself. Successful athletes, scholars, and winners of all types have self-esteem.

In order to have a positive self-image and healthy self-esteem, three things have to occur. First, you must learn important skills, such as the ability to hit a ball well or write an excellent book report. As your skills improve, you gain another important element—confidence. You can control what happens. The more confidence you have, the more skilled you'll become. In other words, these two elements reinforce each other. A third element is responsibility. At some

Learning karate is an excellent way to start on the road to self-esteem, and there are other benefits as well. As you grow as a karate student, you will see growth in other aspects of your life. Karate students are well mannered, strive for high academic performance in school, and have a sense of self-assurance and control that is admired by peers. Now you are ready to learn the karate skills that will, in time, give you the confidence and strength of purpose to greatly improve your life.

Some of the students demonstrating the karate movements shown in this book are: (clockwise from center top) *Robert Wingo, Holly McLeod, Mallice Felder, Heidi McLeod, Sean Kime.*

2

THE WORKOUT

MEDITATION RITUAL

Starting from your very first workout, the first step to do is to learn to perform the meditation ritual. This procedure has nothing to do with religion. You meditate to clear your mind and get in the right mental attitude to begin practice. The ritual is also used to show respect to the art of karate, which you are preparing to learn or take part in, and to your instructor if you are in a class.

The Bow

You begin the meditation ritual with a bow.

To bow properly, first stand erect with your feet close together (the closed stance) and your hands at your sides (**1**). Then, with a stiff and slow movement, bend forward at the waist (**2**). Return to the erect position. The bow is used in many aspects of karate. You will bow at the beginning and at the end of any karate practice whether you work out alone, in a group, or in a formal class. You will also bow at the beginning and end of a kata *(kah-tuh)*, which is a series of pre-arranged moves that start simple and become more complex as you advance in ranks. You will learn about kata in Chapter 6.

In addition to bowing to your instructor at the beginning and ending of class, you bow to your partners at the beginning and end of such exercises as practising self-defense and doing kumite *(koo-muh-tay)*. The bow is always done to show respect for your instructor, partner, or opponent.

1

2

Meditation

After the bow, you move into the meditation stage. Lower your knees to the floor with your legs stretched straight behind. Sit back on your legs and rest your closed fists on your sides, thighs, or on the floor. Close your eyes and tilt your head forward (1). While in the meditation stage, you focus on removing all thoughts and worries from your mind. The goal is to empty the mind in order to focus only on karate. Meditation is difficult in the beginning. All kinds of thoughts will seem to be trying to crowd in. It might help to try imagining a candle burning. Focus on the flame. Watch how it flickers and gracefully moves back and forth. After you learn a punch or a kick, you can replace the candle with an image of a perfect kick or punch. Being able to "see" the movement in all its perfection in your mind's eye is a good way to learn and execute that perfect kick or punch when called upon to do so. In other words, meditation allows you to practise karate techniques in your mind.

1

After you finish meditating, which may take from two to five minutes, you move into the salutation. Salutation is a position showing deep respect to the art of karate or to the instructor. From the meditation position move your body forward to the fullest extent and with arms stretched forward bow your head deeply (2). This salutation, though done slowly and deliberately, lasts no more than thirty seconds. After the salutation, you move back to the meditation stage briefly and then stand up in a ready stance. The ready stance is a basic karate position. The feet are about ten inches apart. The body is erect and the arms are at your sides with fists closed.

2

WARM-UP

After the ritual is completed, you are ready for your warm-up exercises. It is very important to limber up stiff muscles with proper exercises before practising karate, so that you don't hurt yourself. A strained muscle can keep you out of karate practice for weeks. You will also need to do a light series of exercises to cool down after practice. The exercises can be the same, but to cool down you will lower the number of repetitions, do them more slowly, and relax your muscles rather than try to stretch them. This cool-down phase also allows you to control the time it takes for your heart rate to return to normal (similar to the way joggers slow their heart rates gradually after a long run). After the cool down, the session ends with a calming meditation.

Neck Roll

Begin your warm-ups with the upper body exercises and work downwards (top to toe). The first exercise is the neck roll. To do the neck roll, stand erect (**1**) and lower your chin to your upper chest (**2**). As shown, only the head moves. The remainder of the body stands firm and still. From the front position, stretch the neck muscles by moving your head to the left (**3**). Next, circle your head straight back (**4**) and then to the right (**5**). Finish the neck roll by returning your head to the front position. Repeat this exercise ten times. Do the exercise slowly and concentrate on stretching the neck muscles.

1

2

3

5

4

Arm Rolls

Begin this exercise by standing straight up and lifting one arm straight out in front of you (**1**). Next, move your arm straight up and reach as high as you can (**2**). Keeping your body facing front, move your arm behind you and stretch backwards (**3**). Finish the arm roll by circling your arm downwards and return to the first position. Repeat ten times with each arm.

Once each arm has been individually stretched, raise both arms level with your shoulders directly out in front of you and stretch forward (**4**). Begin a circle by lifting your arms straight up overhead (**5**), then straight back behind you (**6**). Finish the circle by returning the arms to the front position (**7**). Repeat ten times. You will continue warming up the upper body by doing the next exercise, known as body bends.

3

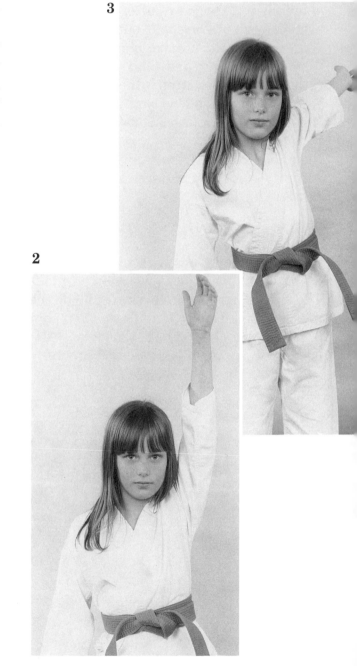

1

2

4

5

Body Bends

Body bends, although continuing to focus on the upper body, also move downwards to include the lower abdomen and the back. To do the body bend, stand erect with your hands resting on your hips. Next, bend your body forward as far as you can stretch (1). Now, bend your body to the right (2), then straight back (3) and to the left (4). Finish the body bend circle by moving back to the front. It is important to keep your legs straight while doing body bends and to stretch as far as you can in each direction. Repeat ten times.

2

1

3

4

Floor Touches

Continuing the stretching down the body, you are now ready to begin warming up the legs. Floor touches are completed in three stages: with the feet placed two or three feet apart, then approximately one foot apart, and finally with the feet together. The purpose of this exercise is to slowly stretch the muscles of the legs to allow you to kick higher and with more power. For stage-one floor touches stand straight with your feet wide apart. Lift your arms and place your hands together to form a triangle (1) with your fingers as shown. Slowly move your body and arms forward and down. It is important here not to bend your knees. As you bend over, try to place the triangle made by your hands on the floor (2). At first this may be difficult, but go as far as you can. Remember, however, do not bounce. Do this ten times. You are now ready for stage two. Place your feet approximately one foot apart (3). Repeat the exercise in the same manner as you did in stage one (4). With your feet closer together, you won't be able to place your hand triangle as close to the floor as you did in stage one. However, this will im-

prove rapidly with time and practice. Do stage-two floor touches ten times, then go to stage three. Bring your feet together (5), raise your arms, and bend downwards as far

Stage One

1

2

Side kicks at head level require good flexibility.

as possible (**6**). Right now you may not get much lower than your knees. With time, however, you will find that you can place the palms of your hands flat on the floor. When that time comes, you will also be throwing side kicks at head levels with great flexibility, power, and speed. Do stage-three floor touches ten times.

3

Stage Two

4

5

Stage Three

6

Toe Lifts

To stretch other muscles in your legs, sit down and place your legs and feet together out in front of you (1). Keeping your legs straight and without bending your knees, reach forward and grab your toes. Lift your feet off the floor and hold for ten seconds (2). Repeat the exercise ten times. The toe lift allows you to stretch muscles from the hips to the lower legs.

Front Leg Bends

Continue stretching the leg muscles with the front leg bend. From ready position, move one leg out in front of you. Keeping your back leg straight, bend your front leg and move your upper body forward as illustrated (3). Next, lower your body over the front leg, which is bent (4). You can rest your hands on the floor lightly to keep your balance. Do five bends with each leg. The second part of this exercise is more difficult. Sit down with one leg stretched out in front of you. Pull your back leg up behind you, as shown, and reach toward your ankles (5).

1

2

3

4

5

6

Keeping the front leg straight and without bending the knee, reach and grab hold of your ankle, or as far down your leg as you can reach. Push your body forward while pulling with your hands (**6**). Do this exercise carefully to avoid straining a muscle. Do five leg bends with each leg. These exercises will stretch the upper and side muscles in your legs and give you greater control over your kicks. Now you need to stretch the muscles on the upper inside of your thighs. This last exercise will give your kicks extra height.

Side Leg Lifts

Stand erect with your feet set about a foot apart (**1**). Slowly lift one leg to the side (**2**). Keep it perfectly straight. Don't bend your knee at all. With each leg lift, try to reach just a little higher (**3**). Soon you'll be able to do leg lifts that reach above your head. Do this exercise ten times with each leg. You are now ready for your first karate lesson.

3

2

1

LESSON ONE

The first karate move you are going to learn is how to deliver a punch from a horse stance to three important targets on the body, so you need to know the right way to make a fist.

The Fist

First, raise both hands up in the air with fingers spread wide (1). Next, press your fingertips tightly against your upper palms (2). Finally, roll your fingers down into your hands and lock them into position with your thumbs, making a tight fist (3). In karate, every body part that can be used for striking out is considered a weapon. The karate fist is rolled much tighter than a person usually does in making a fist. The tighter the fist, the stronger the weapon. The two knuckles shown in the drawing are the striking part of the fist.

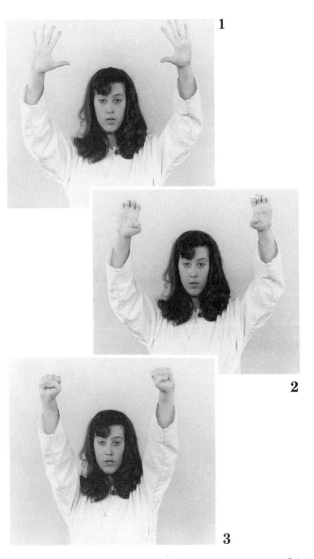

1

2

3

Delivering the Punch

With closed fists thumbside down, push both arms out in front of you at shoulder level (**1**). Next, pull one arm back, turning it so that your fist rests upside down on the side of your hip (**2**). This will seem awkward at first and the position may even feel weak. However, you will quickly discover that your punches are three times stronger than the way you used to punch. Basically, that is because you will be punching in a straight line. There is no wasted motion so it is also faster. Before you started to learn karate, you probably threw a punch by first pulling your fist back behind your back. This put your weight behind the punch, but not your strength or force. Now, to deliver a punch, you simply reverse your hands. The hand in front is pulled back and (**3**) rotated upside down to rest at your hip as the back hand shoots out and rotates (**4**) into a straight fist to strike the target (**5**). The other hand is resting on your hip ready to strike again.

2

1

3

4

Practise punching alternately with each hand. As you do you will see that you are already getting faster. You will also notice how much stronger the punches are beginning to feel to you. One important point to be aware of is to avoid moving your shoulders when you punch. This will strengthen your muscles and focus the arms to push outwards so that they become more forceful with practice.

5

Fighting (Horse) Stance

Next, imagine you are riding a horse. Spread your legs wide and bend your knees deeply, but keep the back straight. Now, raise your hands again while in the horse stance. Open your hands and spread the fingers wide (1), repeating the procedure for making a fist. First fold your fingertips tightly into your upper palms (2) and then roll your hands tightly up into fists (3).

1

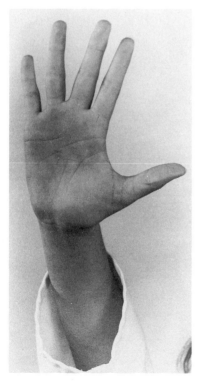

2

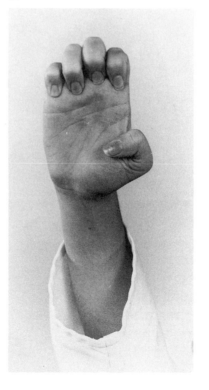

3

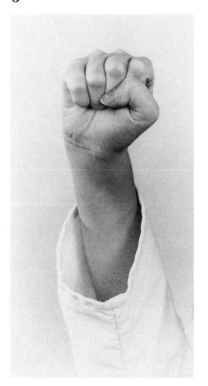

34

Place one hand upside down on your hip and leave the other hand out in front of you (**4**). You are now in a strong fighting stance with a firm foundation. Punch with the hand on your hip as you return the other hand to your hip as you previously learned (**5**). Practise the punches a few times. Now you are ready to strike at the three major targets of the body.

4

5

Hitting the Targets

From the horse stance, deliver a punch to the head area of an opponent (**1**). This is called a rising punch. With the resting hand, punch quickly to the chest area (**2**). This is called a center punch. Just like a machine, each part working in coordination, now move the resting hand and punch to the groin area. This is called a lower punch (**3**).

2

1

3

You have just demonstrated two of the reasons why karate works. One, karate techniques build upon each other and work in sequence. Each part of the body moves at the right time with the desired harmony. Two, the great strength of karate comes from using scientific principles such as a straight line is the shortest distance between two points. For example, a karate punch to the chest of an attacker is much faster than a regular punch that is first pulled behind the body and then delivered. In fact, you will learn that you can throw three punches in the same time that it takes an attacker to throw one.

Going On

I hope that you enjoyed your first lesson. You will learn other karate techniques in the following chapters. Chapter 3 covers more punches and stances. Chapter 4 will show you offensive techniques such as backfist and knifehand in addition to the basic kicks. Chapter 5 will introduce you to defensive karate, and teach you to block and defend yourself against an attacker. Sports karate is covered in Chapter 6. Here you will learn all about the tournaments you can enter to win awards and trophies in kata and kumite. Chapter 7 will answer the most often asked questions about karate. Now, pat yourself on the back for a good start and do some cool-down exercises—the same as warm-ups, but fewer and more slowly. As you do them, concentrate on the movements as your muscles stretch and then relax.

Before your next practice session, think about karate's place in your life. Remember that karate is an art form, a sport, and a means of self-defense. True karate students never go around throwing punches and kicks in public or showing off. This is not the way of karate. Practice karate at home or at a studio with other students, where you can learn the techniques and perfect the art safely, and encourage others to do the same. Most important, act responsibly. Never strike anyone unless you are being attacked and are in danger. If you don't abuse these basic rules, karate will be an enjoyable, confidence-building sport and perhaps may save your life someday.

3

THE BASIC STANCES

In the last chapter you learned the meditation ritual, warm-up exercises, and karate punches. You also learned how to move into a horse stance. In this chapter you are going to learn the basic karate stances.

The stance is the foundation of karate. The form of the karate student is best seen in the stance (1). Look here at the student taking a stance throwing a power punch (2). The strength of the punch comes from the foundation of the stance. Just as a house cannot stand without a solid foundation, neither can a punch, kick, or block endure without a good stance—the building block of karate.

The first stance that you will learn as a karate student is the ready stance.

2

1

Ready Stance

To move into the ready stance, simply stand comfortably with the feet placed approximately ten inches or shoulder-width apart. The knees are slightly relaxed and the fists are held low before you.

The importance of the ready stance is quite obvious. From the ready stance a trained karate expert can move into any karate stance to deliver any kick, block, or punch.

As you begin to learn karate, you will be asked to move into stances and deliver certain kicks or punches. In the beginning you will probably feel somewhat awkward in your movements. But, as you continue to practise on a regular basis, you'll find that the movements will begin to feel more natural and become more graceful. A good analogy is to think of an ice skater. If you have ever tried to ice skate, you know that the first time is very difficult. Simply being able to stand up without falling is a major achievement. However, after some practice you can get around on the ice and, after many years of practice, an Olympics-type skater can do graceful spins, turns, and even triple axles that make it all look so easy. So don't worry about how strange it feels to you now. Soon you will be able to gracefully move from stance to stance and kick to kick without even thinking about it. Each move will come naturally to you, without any wasted time or motion.

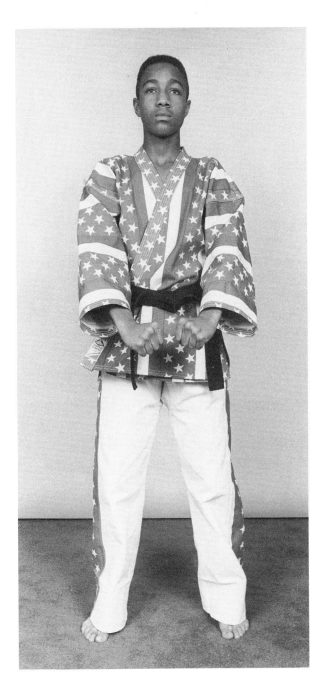

You will find that the first stance in each kata is a ready stance. From that basic position, you move into other stances. The next stance to learn is the front stance.

Front Stance

From a ready stance you can move easily into the front stance. The front stance is one of the strongest stances in karate. It is also the stance you will use most of the time.

To move into a left front stance from a ready stance (**1**), shift most of your weight to your right leg (**2**). While keeping your hands in ready position, slide your left foot (**3**) and leg out to a forward position (**4**). Your back leg remains straight while the left leg is bent at the knee. The drawing shows the correct positioning of the feet. Note that both feet are facing front. The proper distribution of your body weight is over half, actually sixty percent, on the front leg and forty percent on the right leg. To move back into a ready stance, simply reverse the procedure by shifting your weight and sliding your front foot back into the ready stance position. Later you will learn to deliver a powerful front kick from the front stance. Practise moving in and out of the left front stance. To do the right front stance, simply reverse the steps, moving your right foot in front while keeping your left foot behind and straight. Now, your weight is distributed with sixty percent on your right leg and forty percent on your left leg. Practise both variations.

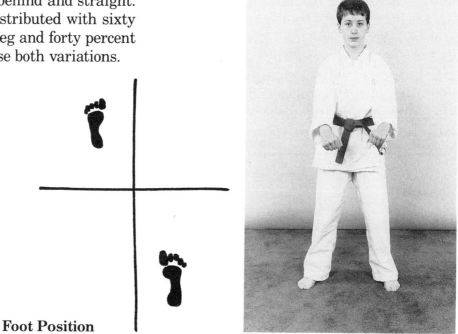

1

Foot Position

42

3

4

2

Back Stance

The opposite of the front stance is the back stance. The back stance will seem awkward to you at first. However, with practice you will begin to see the strength that is obvious in the back stance. From the back stance you can deliver a front kick, side kick, or round-house kick.

From the ready stance (1), move into the right back stance by slightly shifting your weight to the left leg and pulling your right leg in close to the left (2). Then continue to slide your right foot straight back, opening the position of your leg so that your foot points off to the right, or at a right angle to your front leg (3).

In the right back stance your feet are "on line." In other words, a straight line can be drawn from the heel of your front foot to the heel of the right foot. Check to see that your feet are in the right positions as shown in the drawing. Weight distribution in the back stance places seventy percent of your weight on your back leg and only thirty percent on your front leg. In order to get the right balance in the stance, lower your body and shift slightly backwards. The back leg is deeply flexed while the front leg is only slightly bent. To return to the ready stance, shift your weight and reverse your movements. To do a left back stance, move your left leg and foot back in the same manner as you did in the right back stance. Practise both the left and right back stances.

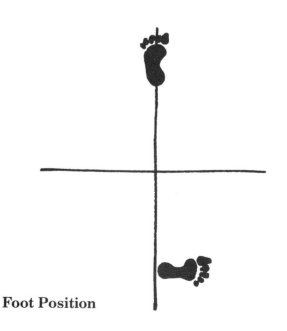

Foot Position

1

2

3

Cat Stance

The cat stance is somewhat similar to the back stance but the emphasis is placed upon keeping the front foot free for most of the kicking. The cat stance resembles a cat crouched ready to strike.

To move into a left cat stance from a ready stance (1), move the left leg forward (2), shifting almost all your weight (ninety percent) onto your back leg while bending the leg deeply. At the same time, move your left foot out as shown and place your foot on the floor with only the ball of the foot touching the floor (3). Only ten percent of your weight is placed on the front foot. The strength of this stance allows you to kick quickly from the front. To do a right cat stance you simply move the right foot out in front. Check the positions of your feet with the drawing here to make sure your cat stance is correct.

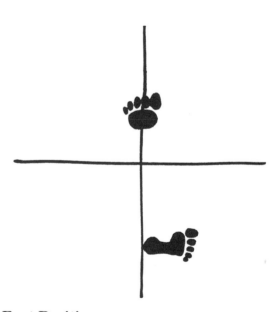

Foot Position

2

1

3

Horse Stance

Earlier you experimented with the horse stance. The horse stance is an extremely strong stance for balance, speed, and power. Any karate kick can be delivered from the horse stance, but the most obvious are the side kick and the roundhouse kick. As you already have learned from your first lesson, the horse stance is excellent for delivering strong punches.

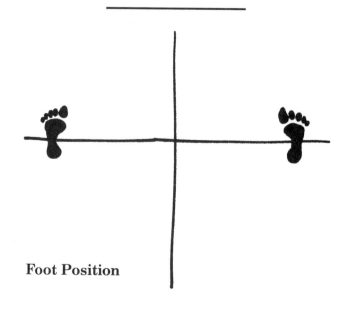

Foot Position

1

To move into a horse stance, shift your weight and slide one foot (**1**) outward, taking a large step. The legs must be spread wide with the knees deeply bent (**2**). In the horse stance, the feet are pointed straight ahead with the heels on line as shown in the drawing. The weight is distributed evenly, fifty percent on the left leg and fifty percent on the right leg. Your body is lowered as you bend your knees deeply.

2

A SOLID FOUNDATION

With practice, and as you incorporate kicks and punches into your routine, you will find that you are able to move from stance to stance almost without thinking about it. For now, these movements are the easiest way to learn to change position quickly. Later, when you practise self-defense, you will learn other ways to move into the various stances. For instance, instead of stepping *up* into a front stance, as you would move toward an attacker at a distance from you, you would step *back* into a front stance, while defending against an attacker who is extremely close. You will experiment with these variations in Chapter 5.

You need to practise these basic stances as much as possible. The karate stance is the foundation of karate. Every other aspect of karate is based upon the stances. Once the stances are learned, much of the other karate fundamentals will follow more easily. Just as it is important to build a solid foundation for a house before putting up the rest of the structure, the stances must be perfected to truly master the art of karate. You are now ready to learn the offensive skills and principles of karate.

4

OFFENSIVE KARATE

In the last chapter you learned the foundation of karate—the stance. You also learned how to properly close your fists and deliver punches at the head, chest, and groin levels. Now you are ready to learn the basic offensive techniques of karate. Remember that the only time you would actually strike another person is when you are being attacked and your life is in danger. At this level it is important to forget about what you have seen on television or in videos, where contact is actually made (or looks as if it is). These actors and stunt people are karate masters who have devoted many years to studying and practising karate. These experts have excellent focus and control over their kicks and punches and are capable of striking out without actually hurting their adversaries. You too will be able to do this someday if you continue to study and practise hard. For now, you must focus your kicks and punches two or three inches from the target. This is especially true if you are practising with a friend or partner.

Backfist Strike

ON THE ATTACK

You are now ready to be introduced to the backfist strike, shuto, reverse punch, front kick, side kick, and roundhouse kick. Read the directions and look at the photographs and drawings carefully before practising these offensive movements.

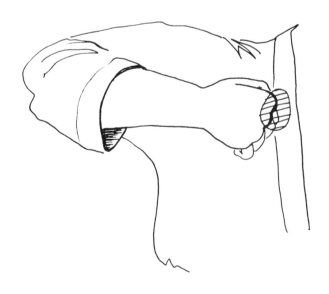

As you can see in the illustrations, the first two knuckles of the back of the hand are used for striking. To learn and practise the backfist, move into a horse stance. Pull your arm across your chest with your fist close to the body. Your arm should be parallel to the floor (1). As you begin to strike, move your forearm in a straight line toward the target while keeping your elbow still. Continue moving your arm and backfist outward until you reach the target (2). After the strike, like a whip recoil your arm and fist back to your chest (3). In other words, reverse the strike route of the backfist at the same speed as it was thrown. As you continue to practise, work for speed. The strength of the backfist strike is multiplied by the speed of the strike and recoil. This procedure is technically called a "snap" because the fist is snapped out and back quickly. If you have ever played in the showers with a towel, using it like a whip, you know there is little power in the strike unless the towel is snapped back. This principle applies to the backfist and many of the other techniques that you will learn in karate. Practise the backfist every time you work out. Major striking areas for the backfist are the temples at the sides of the head, the chest, or the groin. Practise the backfist with both the left and right hands. This technique is one of the easiest to master.

1

2

3

The Shuto

The shuto *(shoe-toe)* is thrown with the bottom of the hand, as shown in the drawing. Karate masters often call this strike a "knifehand." Lay people usually refer to the shuto as a karate chop. The term knifehand, however, is the appropriate one as this strike is actually a snap with the knife edge of the hand. The shuto is basically used to strike at the vulnerable neck and temple areas.

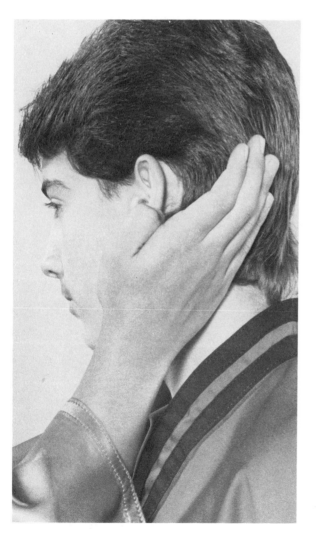

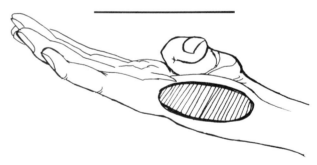

To learn the shuto, move into a right back stance and hold the left arm up as a guard with the hand open and locked and with your right hand open and tucked tightly against your side (1). Pull your right arm up and place it behind the back of your head (2). Shift your body around as you strike with the opened edge of your hand (3). Note that the hand is slightly bent as you strike the target. The arm and hand should be snapped back to the original position, as you did with the backfist. The shuto can be a

1

2

3

Reverse Punch

The reverse punch is different from the regular punch. In the regular karate punch, the hand is not snapped back; while in the reverse punch, it is. The snapping action, the same reason that the backfist and the shuto are so strong, also makes the reverse punch more powerful. The reverse punch can be faster than the regular punch too.

To use the reverse punch, get into a right back stance and place your left hand in front of you as a guard. The hand can be opened or closed (**1**). Quickly push forward and punch with your right hand as your left hand comes in to guard your face (**2**). As soon as you make contact with the target, snap the hand back to your body (**3**). In kumite or sparring competition, perhaps no other technique scores more points than the reverse punch. You are now ready to learn the karate kicks.

1

56

Front Snap Kick

Look at the photographs and the drawing to see how the front kick is done. As you can see, it is the ball of the foot that strikes the target. Remember to pull your toes back out of harm's way as shown.

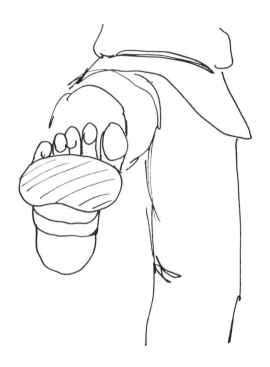

To perform the front snap kick, get into a left front stance and lift your right knee up as you prepare to kick. Keep your hands in front of you to guard your body (1). Execute the front snap kick by extending your foot to the target (2). On contact, snap the foot back to the bent-knee position. Return to a front stance. Practise with both the left and right legs. The front kick can be thrown to the head, body, or groin areas.

1

In a karate class, often the sensei *(sensay)*, or teacher, will guide you to kick with greater force to build strength. Perhaps you can get a parent or friend to help coach you as you practise the front kick. Keep in mind that the legs are three times as powerful as the arms, so your kicks will be much stronger than your punches. You want your kicks to be as strong as possible in case you are attacked by a much larger person.

2

Power Side Kick

Often called the side thrust kick, the power side kick is the strongest kick in karate. If thrown correctly, you could easily knock down an opponent twice your size. From a right back stance keep your hands up for protection and prepare to kick (**1**). Bring your right leg up with your knee to your waist level (**2**). Now spin your body slightly to your left and thrust your foot out, striking the target with your heel (**3**). The leg is not snapped back until the full force of your kick is delivered.

1

2

3

The strength of this kick comes from the power of all your weight as you spin around and drive your foot outward. The side kick can be thrown to the head or body. Practise the kick with both legs.

Side Snap Kick

The side snap kick is much different from the power side kick. This kick is designed to strike quickly to either your left or right sides. To learn the kick, move into either a wider ready stance or a horse stance (**1**).

As you prepare to kick, bring your kicking leg inward with your foot resting on the opposite knee. Pull your hands up in front for protection (**2**). Snap the kick outward to your side, shifting your weight to the non-kicking leg. It is the outside edge of the foot that strikes the target (**3**). As soon as the foot makes contact, snap the leg back to the bent-knee position. The side snap kick can strike both the body and head areas. Practise with both legs.

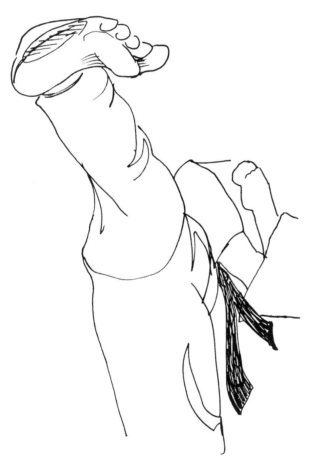

1

62

Roundhouse Kick

Perhaps one of the best kicks a beginner can learn is the roundhouse kick. In this kick you practise balance, speed, and power. The roundhouse kick is a snap kick with the ball of the foot used for striking. The non-kicking foot pivots and turns as the kick is delivered. To learn and practise the roundhouse kick, move into a left front stance and hold your hands in front of you for protection (**1**).

From the front stance, bring your right leg straight up parallel to the floor, placing your foot in position near your hip (**2**). Next, pivot on your left foot, swinging your right leg to the front with the knee high and your upper leg perpendicular to the floor. The toes are pulled back in preparation for the kick (**3**). From this position, snap the leg outward and around while completing the pivot and deliver the kick in a snapping motion (**4**). The foot is recoiled back to the hip for maximum effect.

2

1

4

3

In the beginning, you will have to do this kick in steps as presented, perhaps stopping at each stage. In time, however, with much practice, your kicks will become fluid, going through each stage without pausing.

Practise all your kicks daily and, before you know it, you will be throwing kicks with good form, power, and speed. Remember, always practise each kick with both the left and the right legs.

You have now learned the basic karate offensive techniques. Next you will learn the defensive techniques of blocking and discover how the defensive techniques work in harmony with offensive karate for self-defense.

5

DEFENSIVE KARATE

In the last chapter, you learned attack techniques; now you are going to learn how to defend against an attacker. The best way to learn self-defense is to work with a partner, perhaps another student or a friend or relative. Practising defensive techniques in this manner is called ippon-kumite *(ee-pon koo-muh-tay)*.

Before starting to practise, stand with your feet together facing your partner and measure the reach of your punch to within a few inches of the target (**1**). Now, step back into a left front stance with your left hand in a lower block position (**2**). This is the traditional position that karate students use to practise ippon-kumite. From this position you can practise any self-defense technique as your partner delivers prearrranged kicks or punches for you to defend against and then counter with offensive techniques. As you practise these techniques on a regular basis, you will find that your timing, form, and speed will improve greatly. Remember, you must be careful never to actually strike your training partner. Learn to control your kicks and punches to stop within two inches of the target. Of course, in an actual attack upon your life, you would not stop them but use these same offensive techniques with full force. As you master karate's defensive and offensive techniques, self-defense will come naturally. You will not need to think of stances and movements. Karate will become a part of you and you will simply react automatically to any situation. But that mastering of karate requires many years of practice. Are you ready to begin? If so, get a partner and go through all of the combinations presented in this chapter. Proceed carefully. You may want to work on the first few sequences several times, and add others as you feel more comfortable.

1

2

IPPON-KUMITE

Look at illustration **2** of the photo sequence again and have your partner get into a front stance as shown on the right. After your partner measures the distance of his or her punch and returns to a front stance, signal your partner to throw a punch. Your feet are together and your hands are at your sides. Your partner steps into a right center punch by sliding the right foot into a right front stance and the hands are rotating for a right punch (**3**). As your partner extends the punch to your head, look at the way the right hand and right leg are locked into position (**4**). Notice that the left hand is ready to punch or the left leg is ready to kick. Practise taking turns with your partner being the attacker and the target.

3

4

Upper Rising Block

The rising block is used to block a downwards strike to the head. In many karate blocks, the blocking hand is brought from the front of the body. This is true for the rising block.

As you see your partner's arm coming downwards in a hammer strike, move into a right forward stance while bringing your right arm up across your body (**1**). Continue moving into the right front stance and complete your rising block at the same time (**2**). Notice that the arm is raised over the head area and turned outward. The blocking part of the arm is the outside edge of the arm.

Remember, you can move either towards your opponent, as shown in the sequence here, or you can move back into a front stance if the opponent is close to you when striking.

1

Outside Center Block

Perhaps the strongest karate block is the outside center block. This block comes from the outside to the center of your body to fend off punches and kicks to the chest area.

To do the block, move into a left front stance with your right arm and fist lifted and turned behind your head (**1**). With one swift move, bring your arm around and down across your body to block (**2**). The side-view sequence here shows clearly this preparation of the block (**3**) and then the turn (**4**). The block is completed with the side of the arm serving as the blocking area as you can see in the photo at right.

1

2

3

4

Lower Block

The lower block is used most often to block a kick to the lower part of the body. You can learn the lower block by moving into a left front stance and pulling your arm and fist (palmside inward) around to the right side of your head (**1**). To complete the block, simply turn your arm and bring it straight down, blocking with the outside edge of the arm (**2**).

1

2

In the side view you can see the preparation for the lower block (3). Finish the block as shown in the photo at left. Once you get used to the arm movements in the blocks, you can work on timing the blocks to make contact at the same time you lock into your stance.

3

Remember to practise the blocks using both the left and right arms in turn. In the beginning, move from a ready stance to block with the left arm as you move into a left front stance. As you move from a ready stance to block with the right arm, you will use the right front stance. As you master the techniques, using these matched movements will not be as important.

Inside Center Block

When you use the inside center block you are using a weaker but very effective block. To learn this block, in a right front stance simply move the right hand from a bent-arm position (1) to a straight-up position (2). The block is done with the outside part of your arm as you can see in the photograph at right. One of the strengths of this block is that it is in close and a fast counterpunch can be thrown immediately with the resting hand (3).

In fact, after each block, the resting hand is always ready to punch, block, or strike offensively.

1

2

3

Practise all of the above blocks and immediately counter by delivering a punch to either the head and body areas. You will also discover that, as you block with the left hand and then punch with the right, the left hand is ready to punch again—then the right—then the left. Get the idea? If so, you now understand how the techniques of karate work scientifically to establish a system of self-defense.

You are now ready to work more advanced sequences of self-defense.

BLOCK AND COUNTER

Body Punch Counter

In this exercise, block your partner's right punch to the chest with a left inside center block (**1**). Step in with a right front stance and deliver a right punch to the body (**2**).

1

2

Head Punch Counter

Use a left lower block in a left stance as you block a kick to the groin area (1). Immediately deliver a right punch to the head as you move into a right front stance (2).

Don't forget to practise the exercises using both the left and right sides of the body.

1

2

Backfist Counter

This sequence provides practice in the horse stance as you block a kick. From a ready stance, step back into a horse stance and use a right lower block to ward off your partner's right side kick (1). Immediately, lean forward in your stance and deliver a right backfist (2).

1

2

Center Punch Counter

Step back into a left front stance and use a left inside center block to stop a right roundhouse kick to the head (1). Step up into a right front stance and deliver a right center punch (2).

1

2

Front-Kick Punch Counter

In this sequence you will be striking back twice. Block a hammer block with a left upper block in a left front stance (1). Keep your block up and deliver a right front kick to the stomach (2). After the kick, drop the foot down into a right front stance (since your kick knocks the opponent back) and deliver at the same time a right front punch to the body (3).

1

2

3

Snap-Kick Punch Counter

You will continue with the combinations of strikes. Use a right outside center block to stop a punch (**1**). Lift the right leg, turn, and deliver a side snap kick to the body (**2**). To gain more power in your punch, shift to the left hand in a right front stance and deliver a punch to the head (**3**).

1

3

2

Double-Kick Counter

Now experiment with using two kicks after you block. Block a lower block to the groin (1). Lift your right leg from the front stance and deliver a right roundhouse kick to the head area (2). Since the opponent has been knocked back, bring the right leg around and throw a power side kick to the stomach (3).

1

3

2

Double-Kick Backfist Counter

Block a right roundhouse kick with a left inside center block (**1**). From your right front stance deliver a front kick to the body (**2**). Step down into a left front stance and throw a right power side kick to the stomach (**3**). Come down into a horse stance and throw a right backfist to the head (**4**).

2

1

4

3

Kick Roundhouse Counter

From a left back stance, use a right inside center block to stop a front kick to the body (**1**). Execute a hard front kick to the body (**2**). Step your kick into a left front stance and throw a right roundhouse to the head area (**3**).

Practise these combinations every time you work out with a partner.

1

2

3

WARNING! Learn to deliver your offensive technique quickly after the block. Like you, your attacker has more than one weapon. Here is what can happen if you are too slow with your strike after the block. Suppose you successfully block a front kick with a center block in a left back stance (**1**). If you are too slow, your attacker can move quickly and hit you with a kick or punch before you can strike (**2**). So learn the movements and practise for speed; but, be careful. As you practise to be fast you run a greater risk of unintentionally hitting your partner with an uncontrolled punch or kick. At first, when you are practising for speed, make your focus point *at least four inches* from the target. Then, as your speed and control improve, you can move back to the two-inch focus point.

Practise numerous combinations, the ones above as well as those of your own design. Also, do ippon-kumite with as many different partners as possible. This will give you more practice adjusting to the different sizes, sparring distances, and speeds of your opposing partners. Just remember always to be careful.

2

1

6

SPORTS KARATE

Now that you have learned the basic principles and how to put combinations of karate blocks, kicks, and punches together for self-defense, you can compete in tournaments to win trophies and prizes.

Karate tournaments are held at local, state, regional, national, and international levels all over the world. There is a good chance that at least one tournament is being held annually within a fifty-mile radius of your home.

Competition is the heart of sports karate and you will find most tournaments to have a welcoming and friendly atmosphere. Martial artists love to socialize and make new friends. Although pleasant in spirit, competition is usually tough and extremely demanding. Winners of most tournaments are usually individuals who are serious and devoted students of karate. They practise for long hours daily and enter competitions frequently.

Tournament karate is usually divided by age, size, sex, and rank. A division for children under six years of age is not uncommon. Often there is a division for five- and six-year-old students. Typically, in kumite, boys compete with boys and girls with girls. In kata competition, boys and girls compete together except in the highest ranks. Size plays an important role in divisions under twelve years of age, but after that age a student's rank takes priority. Ideally, age, size, sex, and rank should be equal and well balanced. However, many times a higher-ranking division will have too few contestants so the students are forced to compete above their level or against larger students. Often there is no other way that will allow the students who want to do so to compete.

A person does not have to enter tournaments, however, to be a great martial artist. Many top karate masters of yesterday and today never entered tournaments. Too, a lot of serious students of karate find tournaments to be overwhelming or too "sports" oriented for them. Other artists consider the judging at tournaments to be inconsistent or unfair, so don't compete. In any event, it will help you to have a clear understanding of sports karate whether you work out alone, with a friend, or take part in a tournament. Kumite, or free-style sparring, and kata are major elements in both the art and the sport of karate. In time, you will decide whether you want to focus more on karate as an art form, sport, or both.

Rank is divided into four major divisions: beginner, intermediate, advanced, and expert.

Karate students are identified by the colored belts they wear. A beginner starts out with a white belt and usually advances to yellow and then orange. No time limit is involved in this promotion. Belt colors are awarded upon mastery of certain skills that determine the level achieved. Students progress at different rates based upon varying amounts of instructional time, practice, and natural ability.

On an average, competitors in the beginners' divisions have studied karate from three to eighteen months. Since these are usually the largest divisions, many instructors believe that the beginning division should be further divided into two or three divisions, corresponding to the first, second, and third belts. Unfortunately, you may find yourself, as a white belt with three months of training, competing in kumite and kata with a student wearing an orange belt, who has had a year or more of practice and training.

In the intermediate divisions, you will find competitors who have practised karate from one to three years. These contestants wear a green, blue, or purple belt. Known as the green belt division, these students take karate seriously, putting in the time and effort to advance. Only about one-fourth of the students taking karate ever make it to this level. This is not because of ability, but simply due to the lack of dedication to the art or sport. In other words, they quit before reaching this level. Make yourself a promise now to work hard to get to the green-belt level and your chances of becoming a black belt are significantly improved.

At the advanced level are the brown belt divisions. Although there are often only a few students in each of the brown belt divisions, the competition is fierce and highly challenging. Most brown belts are hungry for the black belt and in this level strive to impress their instructors.

Finally, there is the black-belt, or the expert, level. Achieving the black belt is the major goal of any serious karate student. On an average, it takes anywhere from four to seven years of intense study to reach the level of mastery required to receive the black belt. Set your sights for the black belt—make it your goal!

To begin sparring or kumite you will need some basic equipment. In addition to a karate suit, or gi, you will need a mouthpiece, cup athletic supporter (boys) or breast protector (girls), belt, and gloves for the hands and feet. These can usually be purchased from a karate instructor or ordered from a company advertising in karate magazines.

Equipment for sparring is needed to protect you and your opponent. Most tournament officials require students twelve and under to also wear headgear.

Once you have paid your fees and been assigned to a division, you are ready to participate. You will be competing for awards such as cash, savings bonds, and trophies. These are usually awarded to the top four

contestants in each division. Some first-place trophies are six feet tall. Quite impressive!

Once registration is completed, the contestants come together for a formal "rules meeting." This is important because a few rules may vary from tournament to tournament; however, most rules are similar. After the official bowing to the director of the tournament, rules for kumite and kata are reviewed and demonstrated. Most of the rules include scoring, sportsmanship, and safety.

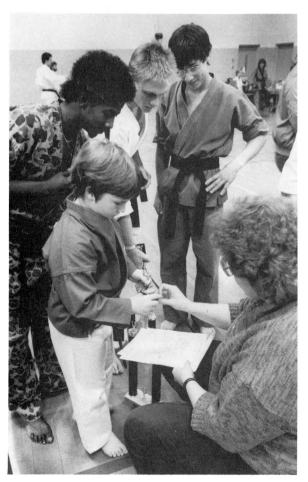

KUMITE

Kumite is known as free-style sparring. In kumite you use kicks and punches to score points against your opponent. You use blocks to stop your opponent's kicks and punches from scoring (**1**). To score a point you must deliver an unblocked kick or punch to the head or body of your opponent (**2**). The labelled illustrations on the opposite page show the areas to strike in order to earn points. In some tournaments, the rule is that karate techniques cannot be thrown to the groin, neck or kidney areas. A kick, strike, or punch that is not blocked, but delivered with control and focus, scores one point.

The winner is determined by the number of points awarded. The student who scores the highest number of points during the two-minutes match wins. A student can also win if he is the first to score a total of three points. Some matches require a total of five points. Additionally, in some tournaments, kicks earn more points than punches. You need to pay close attention to the rules. It is best if you can get a set of rules in advance of the tournament so that you can practise with the rules in mind.

1

2

Major Target Areas

HEAD — FACE

THROAT

CHEST AREA

ABDOMEN

GROIN AREA

NECK

BACK AREA

KIDNEYS

To begin the kumite match, you and your opponent face the center judge and bow (1). Next, you face each other and bow. The judge will then direct you to get into position and will shout "Begin," "Fight," or "Kumite." You're now on your own (2). But, before you begin kumite, be aware of your surroundings. You are standing in a taped-off, 20 by 20 foot square. There is a center judge and two to four corner judges. Points are awarded by the center judge when a majority of the judges see a kick, strike, or punch score. For example, two of three judges must vote on the scoring technique in order to award the point.

1

2

When it appears that a point has been scored, any judge can call for the center judge to stop the match. The time clock is stopped and the judges vote by pointing to the contestant they believe scored (**1**).

If a judge believes no point was earned, the hands are crossed downwards (**2**). If the judge did not see the technique (such as if your back was to that judge) the hand is placed over the eyes, indicating a disqualification from voting (**3**).

1

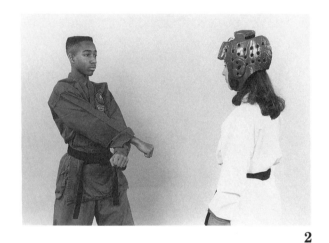

2

3

Points can also be awarded to you because of your opponent's inappropriate contact, unsportsmanlike conduct, or disrespect to a judge. The center judge can disqualify any contestant for the above infractions. Never argue with a judge. It is impolite and shows a lack of self-discipline.

Now you are ready to kumite. The referee or center judge begins the match. You are sparring.

You may find kumite difficult at first. Kumite requires timing, speed, and control. Remember, you don't actually make contact here—even if you are wearing gloves. Most tournaments, however, allow light contact.

It is only in some tournaments, especially for older students in higher ranks, that contact is required. Whenever you spar, however, always be careful!

To begin learning kumite, you must learn to combine your techniques as you did with the defensive techniques you learned in Chapter 5. However, this time your opponent will not be standing still and can block and strike just as you block and strike.

Kumite Techniques

There is no specific order you should follow in using punches, kicks, or strikes in kumite, but it will help in the beginning to practise some of the sequences below with a partner to become more comfortable with free-style sparring.

To become a top kumite competitor, you must develop your own combinations of techniques and learn to execute them with speed, control, and accuracy. In the meantime, these seven sequences will help you practise:

Technique 1: You throw a backfist to your opponent's face, which is blocked (**1**). You immediately counter with a punch to your opponent's face for the point (**2**).

1

2

Technique 2: Again you throw a backfist to your opponent's head, which is blocked (3). You execute a right side kick to your opponent's stomach area (4).

3

4

5

Technique 3: You deliver a backfist as a fake to catch your opponent off guard (**5**). You throw a roundhouse kick to your opponent, which is blocked (**6**). To score, you immediately deliver a right punch to the center of your opponent's body (**7**).

6

7

Technique 4: You throw a right side kick, which your opponent blocks (**8**). Your opponent attempts to strike you with a punch, which you block with a rising block (**9**). While keeping your block up you deliver a center punch to the body for the score (**10**).

10

9

8

103

Technique 5: Your opponent throws a side kick to your body, which you block with a lower block (**11**). You step in to strike with a backfist to your opponent's head (**12**). You are awarded a point by the judges (**13**).

11

12

13

14

Technique 6: Often a simple exchange of techniques scores a point. Your opponent throws a front kick to your lower body. You block the kick (**14**). You counter immediately with a front kick to score on your opponent (**15**).

15

Technique 7: You deliver a front kick to your opponent, which is blocked with a lower block (**16**). You throw a punch with your left hand, which is blocked with a center block (**17**). To score, you throw a right punch to the head (**18**).

16

17

18

As previously stated, you need to practise a number of combinations of kicks and punches. Practise blocking and countering with punches and kicks. Most important, as you practise kumite, be sure to remember to keep moving as you spar.

Many times you can avoid being scored on by simply moving to the side or back as your opponent strikes. As you become more advanced, you will be able to feint or fake out your opponent and strike as the punch or kick misses.

KATA

Kata is considered the most beautiful part of karate. It is actually why karate is seen as an art form. A kata is composed of a series of prearranged karate moves which, when performed, look like a kind of dance.

Kata movements can be beautiful and quite graceful. Katas also allow you to practise your kicks and punches in a prescribed pattern according to rank. In fact, katas are practised for performance in order to advance. You will have to perform specific katas well to be awarded a higher belt. For example, to receive the yellow belt, you would have to perform Heian *(hay-on)* One and Heian Two.

Katas were originally developed by the old masters from the Orient, but new katas have also been created by today's karate masters. The katas are made up of combinations of blocks, kicks, and punches most often forming patterns of movement. These patterns, a straight line, an angle, the letter H, and so on, are best seen from overhead— a bird's-eye view. Some of the more advanced katas resemble certain animal movements such as those of the tiger, snake, or crane. Katas are judged by accuracy, power, form, and speed. Some katas focus more on power, while other katas are designed to demonstrate speed. At the advanced levels, katas include all of the elements. Most beginning katas focus on form and power.

At a karate tournament, katas are performed in front of a total of three or five judges. You are judged and given a score ranging between one and ten. Ten is the highest score. To avoid ties, most tournaments use a decimal system such as 3.1, 6.4, etc., to score katas.

As you approach the judges you bow (**1**) and then stand and announce your name and the name of your kata (**2**). Ask for permission to begin and then start performing your kata (**3**).

You are now ready to learn your first kata. This kata has been especially designed for you, the beginning student, to practise and perform most of the techniques you have learned in this book. The kata is called Basic Kata One.

1

2

3

Basic Kata One

Stand in a ready stance to prepare (**1**).

Bow to the judges in a closed stance with your feet together (**2**).

1

2

Deliver a left lower block in a left front stance (3).

From the left front stance, execute a right front kick to waist level (4).

Return your right foot to the left front stance and deliver a right punch to the head level (5).

Follow your right punch with a left punch to the head (**6**).

Turn 90 degrees to your left and execute a left rising block in a left front stance (**7**).

6

7

Bring the right leg around and throw a power side kick (**8**).

Return to a left front stance and deliver a right center punch (**9**).

Slide the left leg into the right leg while turning to face the judges. Notice that the right hand is held over the left hand (**10**), (**11**).

From this closed position, execute a right snap kick with the right arm held over the hand for balance (**12**).

9

8

10

11

12

Step down from the right side kick into a horse stance and prepare to deliver a right backfist (**13**).

Execute the right backfist (**14**).

Move the left leg toward the right leg (**15**).

Place your left fist over your right hand and close your feet together (**16**).

Turn quickly to your left and execute a left shuto strike while in a right back stance (**17**).

15

16

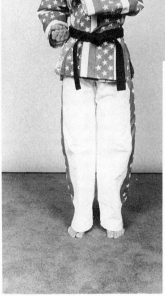

17

Shift into a left front stance and throw a shuto strike with your right hand to the neck area (**18**).

Without moving the position of your feet, turn your body another 90 degrees back to the front into a right front stance and deliver a right lower block (**19**).

Drop to your left knee and deliver a left punch to the groin level (**20**).

20

19

18

Stand up and draw the left leg into the right leg while you bring both arms to your side (**21**).

Close your body up into a closed stance with your feet together and your hands touching your sides as you finish your kata with a formal bow to the judges (**22**).

22

21

You have finished the kata. Practise this kata daily and work to improve your balance, power, and form. This kata is not designed to be done quickly. Perform it slowly and concentrate on good form and power.

You probably have some questions that you would like answered about karate. In Chapter 7 you will find the answers to some of the most often asked questions about karate.

7

QUESTIONS & ANSWERS

Q: At what age should I begin karate?

A: There is no best age to start, but students younger than five years of age may have difficulty with the exercises and karate techniques. All ages, from six years old and up, can benefit and do well in karate.

Q: What will I need to begin karate?

A: All you really need is some loose clothing such as a sweat suit or loose jeans. However, you can order a gi, or karate suit, from companies advertising in some of the popular karate magazines. You also need an area big enough to do your karate and kumite practice. A large room, garage, or backyard will usually do.

Q: Do I need a karate instructor?

A: You can learn more about karate working with a karate instructor. The instruction found in this book, however, is adequate for the beginner. You will need an instructor to advance to the intermediate levels.

Q: How do I find a karate instructor?

A: Check in the yellow pages of your local telephone book to see if there are any karate clubs or schools in your area. You might contact the YMCA or YWCA to see if classes are offered. Also some athletic clubs and even public schools have classes in the afternoons or evenings. Be sure to talk with students of the club to see if the instructor has separate classes for your age group. Ask your parents to check with the Better Business Bureau to make sure the instructor follows good business practices. The instructor should also be at least a first-degree black belt or higher.

Q: What do karate classes cost?

A: That varies from place to place and with the number of lessons offered each week. Most instructors teach karate as a second job and more for enjoyment than for profit. However, for two lessons each week, you should expect to pay anywhere from $50 to $80 dollars per month. Avoid instructors who make you pay large sums to join the club, or offer a black belt program, or a one-time fee. These costs can easily run into the hundreds and even thousands of dollars. Most instructors will allow you to visit a few classes before you join. Watch how the instructor works with the students. Avoid instructors who scream at their students or make students do excessive exercises for disciplinary reasons. Ask the students how they feel about the classes.

Sensei J. Allen Queen (top center) *with a class of his karate students.*

Q: How do I find out about karate tournaments?

A: Most tournaments are advertised in karate magazines. Perhaps the best source for information on tournaments, rankings, costs, etc., is *Sport Karate International*, which is the official publication of the National Blackbelt League. The address of the publication is: Smash Publications, Sport Karate International Magazine, 341 East Fairmount Avenue, Lakewood, NY 14750.

Q: Is all karate the same?

A: There are numerous styles of karate that were designed by different masters. Most styles of karate come from the Orient: Japan, China, Okinawa, and Korea. They are usually similar but require different katas for rank. Korean karate calls for more kicks than Japanese karate, for example. Some styles are "softer," with smooth and graceful movements while other, so-called harder, styles are performed with sharper, more angular moves. There is no superior style.

Q: Can the study of karate affect my school grades?

A: Yes, karate students often find their grades improve. What happens is that as you become more disciplined and more focused in karate and take on more responsibility for your actions, those qualities spill over into your handling of schoolwork.

Q: Why should I study karate?

A: Unlike team sports, karate not only gives you the opportunity to expand your physical and mental skills, but to put them to use in self-defense. With the sport of karate, you can enter and compete in tournaments for prizes and trophies. You can also learn to practise karate as an art.

Q: Do karate students have to register their hands?

A: No, that is one of the myths surrounding the study of karate. Karate does not give you superhuman strength that is a danger to others—you simply learn to maximize all your potential when you punch or kick. Another myth is that you can get a black belt in six months. Wrong. It takes anywhere from four to seven years to become a black belt.

Q: Will karate study help me in other sports?

A: Absolutely. The stretching and physical exercises as well as the mental discipline required in the study of karate should help you to perform better in any sport that you undertake.

ABOUT THE AUTHOR

J. Allen Queen was born in Lincoln County, North Carolina, and graduated from West Lincoln High School in 1969. He earned a B.S. and an M.A. degree, both in Elementary Education, at Western Carolina University, completing the doctoral program in education at the University of Virginia in 1978.

Presently a professor in the School of Education at the University of North Carolina at Charlotte, Dr. Queen has served as a Principal in the Charlotte-Mecklenburg Schools, as Principal with Kings Mountain Schools, as Chairman of the Department of Education at Gardner-Webb College, and as a classroom teacher.

J. Allen Queen's interest in karate is long-standing; he has studied karate for over twenty-five years and has been an instructor for close to twenty years. Holder of a fifth-degree black belt, he currently teaches karate only in seminars and special classes.

Queen is the author of five books on karate, all specifically written for elementary and junior-high school students. His works have been published in the United States, Canada, Europe, and Australia.

Dr. Queen, his wife, Patsy, and their son, Alexander, currently live in Kings Mountain, North Carolina.

INDEX

A
Advertisements, for tournaments, 124
Age, starting, 122
Arm rolls, 22–23
Attacking, 52–65

B
Backfist counter, 80
Backfist strike, 52–53
Back stance, 44–45
Basic kata one, 111–119
Beginner division, 94
Beginning requirements, 122
Belt colors, 94
Black belts, 94
Blocks
    counters for. *See* Counters
    inside center, 76–77
    lower, 74–75
    outside center, 72–73
    practicing, warning for, 89
    upper rising, 70–71
Body bends, 24–25
Body punch counter, 78
Bow, 19
Brown belt division, 94

C
Cat stance, 46–47
Center punch counter, 81
Clothing, 11–12, 122
Cool-down, 38. *See also* Warm-up exercises
Cost, of classes, 123
Counters
    backfist, 80
    body punch, 78
    center punch, 81
    double-kick, 84–85
    double-kick backfist, 86–87
    front-kick punch, 82
    head punch, 79
    kick roundhouse, 88
    practising, warning for, 89
    snap-kick punch, 83

D
Defensive karate, 68–89
Delivering the punch, 32–33

Double-kick backfist counter, 86–87
Double-kick counter, 84–85

E
Equipment, for kumite or sparring, 94

F
Fighting stance, 34–35
Fist, 29
Floor touches, 26–27
Foot position
    for back stance, 44
    for cat stance, 46
    for front stance, 42
    for horse stance, 48
Front-kick punch counter, 82
Front leg bends, 30–31
Front snap kick, 58–59
Front stance, 42–43

G
Gi, 11–12, 94
Green belt division, 94

H
Hands, of karate students, 124
Head punch counter, 79
Heian one and two, 108
Hitting targets, 36–37
Horse stance, 34–35, 48–49

I
Inside center block, 76–77
Instructors, 59, 122–123
Ippon-kumite, 68–69

J
Japanese karate, 124

K
Karate
    defensive, 68–89
    instructors, 59, 122–123
    offensive, 52–65
    place in your life, 38
    reasons to study, 124
    rewards of, 10
    sport or tournament, 92–119
Kata, 19, 108–119
Kick roundhouse counter, 88

Kicks
   controlling, 13
   power side, 60–61
   roundhouse, 64–65
   side snap, 62–63
Knifehand, 54–55
Korean karate, 124
Kumite, 93, 96–101
   equipment for, 94
   scoring, 96–99
   techniques, 101–107

L
Lesson one, 29–37
Lower block, 74–75

M
Meditation, 20
Meditation ritual, 18

N
Neck rolls, 21
Nutrition, 13

O
Offensive karate, 52–65
Outside center block, 72–73

P
Power side kick, 60–61
Punches
   controlling, 13
   delivering, 32–33

R
Rankings, 94
Ready stance, 41
Reasons to study karate, 124
Reverse punch, 56–57
Roughage, 13
Roundhouse kick, 64–65
Rules meeting, 95

S
Safety, 12–13, 94
Salutation, 20
School grades, karate and, 124

Scoring
   for kata, 109
   for kumite, 98–99
Self-esteem, 13–14
Sensei, 59
Shuto, 54–55
Side-leg lifts, 28
Side snap kicks, 62–63
Snap, 53
Snap-kick punch counter, 83
Sparring equipment, 94
Sports karate, 92–119
Sports training, karate and, 124
Stances, 40
   back, 44–45
   cat, 46–47
   fighting or horse, 34–35
   front, 42–43
   horse, 48–49
   as solid foundation, 40
Stretching, bouncing, or forcing, 12
Strikes, backfist, 52–53
Styles of karate, 124

T
Target areas, major, 97
Targets, hitting, 36–37
Toe lifts, 30
Tournaments, 92–119, 124
Trophies, 94–95

U
Upper rising block, 70–71

V
Vitamin B, 13
Vitamin C, 13

W
Warm-up exercises, 12, 21
   arm rolls, 22–23
   body bends, 24–25
   floor touches, 26–27
   neck rolls, 21
   side-leg lifts, 28
Water, 13
Workout space, 11, 122